Poetry From an
"Uneducated"
Black Mind

By: Khaalil Sutton

Copyright © 2020 by KC Publishing

All rights reserved. This book or any portion thereof may not be reproduced or used in any manner whatsoever without the express written permission of the publisher except for the use of brief quotations in a book review.

Printed in the United States of America

First Printing, 2020

ISBN: 978-0-578-73750-8

KC Publishing
4007 Carpenter Rd Unit 369
Ypsilanti, MI 48197

(313) 771-9091
www.kushiyacollective.com

Table Of Contents

I	Outside World
II	Guidance
III	Sea Of Thought
IV	Black Fear
V	Smile
VI	Window Pane
VII	Hues
VIII	Sonder
IX	Post Flood
X	575 #1
XI	Love
XII	My Sisters Keeper
XIII	Keeper Of My Sister
XIV	Betrayal
XV	575 #2
XVI	Abandonment
XVII	Asthma
XVIII	I Took A Walk
XIX	White Fear
XX	575 #3
XXI	The Black Love Paradox
XXII	Boredom
XXIII	Heart Cold
XXIV	Royal Black
XXV	The Names

*Dedicated to
The misunderstood
The forgotten
And the forsaken*

<><><><><><><><>

Outside World

That first step
The one that starts it all
Direct and straight to the point
No B.S.
One intention
Ready for whatever
Every moment before this is obsolete
The final goodbye to a previous life
><><><><><><><><><><><
I

Guidance

Is it something I need
it's not like I'm a baby, and can't feed
The fact that I've made it this far
should prove that I'm not just sub par
I've got my own mind, thoughts, and opinions
And I'm sorry if I'm hurting your feelings
but there's not much value your words can give me
Your efforts just aren't getting through
you can just tell me if it's something you wanna prove
I bet you think all I hear is a hum
well I wonder where I get it from

<><><><><><><><><><><><><><><><><>

Sea Of Thought

><><><><><><><
Didn't really think about the consequences
now I'm laying in repentance
Wondering what went wrong
my mind feels lost in a fog
I have little direction
like where should I put my affection
It's just the little things y'know
each like a flake that makes up the bigger snow
But we don't get that
coming our way is a RAT A TAT TAT
Every waking moment like a dream
except without all the whips and cream
I want my glass to be half full
but the emptiness has a little more pull
This sea of thoughts tugging at my line
but was I ever fishing in mine?
><><><><><><><><><><><><><><><
III

Black Fear

Is this really "the land of the free" when I'm a slave to my fear
And how could this be home to the brave
When they cower behind that
GOLDEN shield and GUNmetal sword
I see it in their eyes
The determination to spill blood
The blatant bloodlust only for me and my ancestors
Is it safe to assume that they are beyond reason?
Even if this is the wrong mentality to have can you blame me for feeling this way?
I'm tired of crying
I hate falling asleep on a pillow soiled from my tears and feeing the wetness on my face while knowing it's because an "accident" happened
That could've been me
They all could've been me
Just sit and try to imagine yourself dying
Blood rushing out from the freshly opened bullet hole
A cold chill stems from a new orifice
That never seems to go away
Your watery eyes barely able to see the one who did this to you but you still can make out their weapon pointed at your head
Thoughts of your family and friends rush into you mind while you wonder if you deserved that golden ticket

You can faintly hear the ambulance through your
blood clogged ears but you know its too late
All of your dreams, ambitions, and plans are just as
good as the blood that has left your body and entered
the cracks in the pavement, just remnants of your
fading life that will come to an end in the coming
moments
You look up one more time at your killers face and
can see a satisfied smile like they've just stolen the
one that belonged to you
That Is Black Fear

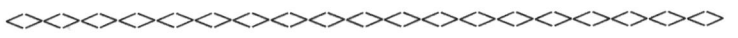

IV

Smile

><><><><

I wonder how I can smile
Even while everywhere I look there's disaster
This expression that consumes my face
It portrays an untruth… it haunts me
I FEAR FOR MY OWN LIFE
Is that selfish?
Is it wrong of me to only be concerned for myself
Or is that just the human condition
I wonder how I can smile
When nobody does the same
Whenever I see a change in those familiar poker faces
it's always through emojis
How will I know love if the deck dealt to me is
devoid of hearts
My outside may be warm and joyful but I can never
purge the chill that fills my body
I wonder how I can smile
While my brother and sisters can't anymore
While they lie in the cold ground… lifeless
AM I NEXT?
Am I waiting to be served like a stuffed pig
on a silver platter
Just another mistake
In the big book of Kappy Klack Kaccidents
><><><><><><><><><><><><><><

Window Pane
Looking through the glass I observe the works of the creator

Sun rays beam down to light the way for the many
animals that call this field their home
The deer while large in stature are gentle with their
steps and seem to calculate each one as if it could
mean life or death
The bird scours the ground for lesser prey than itself
to find a suitable meal
fit for the young ones she has raised
The squirrel lively in nature scurries around the field
as if erratic movements help the memories of last
seasons food which is buried deep underground
take shape
The rabbit always curious sniffs the air
constantly looking for food and danger
simultaneously
The honey bee unknowingly vital swoops from
flower to flower in a dancing like pattern of flight
while helping to ensure a long lineage for each plant
he visits
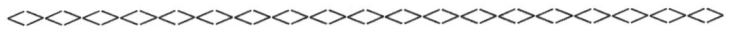

Hues

BLUE
><><><

I can't really explain it
It's like a rush of cool water over my toes while I stare deep into the horizon contemplating the life I've lived
A life that has brought me to this exact moment
I can't really say for sure if it was good or bad
Who am I to decide?
I've only seen the one perspective, the one viewpoint, the one outcome
But I can say I've thoroughly enjoyed the ride

><><><><><><><><><><><><><><><

PURPLE
><><><

I can't really explain it
This felling of euphoria that overwhelms my fragile nerves and subdues my pounding heart into submission
The realization that here in this moment I am me and I'm not afraid to let this vulnerable skin be free for the world to see
Pure bliss

><><><><><><><><><><><><><><><

RED

><><><

I can't really explain it
These desires portray a different version of myself
that has never see a ray of sun
They endlessly pound at my chest for me to let them
out
I can not
If they were to be let free, the side of myself most
acquainted with the world would cease to exist for
the simple fact that
I like it
This cage must hold
and the demons must be kept in check because
I'm not ready for what happens next

VII

Sonder

<><><><><>

   You   You
        You   You
   You   You

Never have I felt like part of the collage
Sitting in place, never out of it
Always there
I was the main character of this book… ME!
Of course I admired the great works of art that summoned my gaze
But was the art always gazing back?
Am I just another pawn in this game of life only moving two steps at a time whilst the unknown queen of foreign origins heads the board?
This paradox of a reality… this false truth where I don't really matter is a remote island that I don't even want to vacation
Is acceptance the key to this mystery lock of collected thoughts or will it just expose another horrid gospel

<><><><><><><><><><><><><><><>

VIII

Post Flood

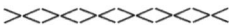

The wells of my eyes run dry as I lay in silence
The monsoon has passed… for now
I know the downpour will be back
As long as the rain clouds loom overhead
As long as mixed emotions flatter my conscious until it gets taken to bed
As long as crowded thoughts swelter the red river in my veins
As long as the cracks in the center of my crore never heal
As long as magma flows through the cracks when new impressions appear
As long as I am me

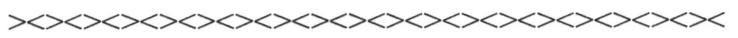

IX

575 #1

The heart red from tears
Colorful in appearance
Never looking deep
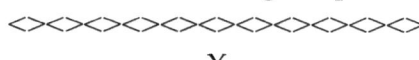
X

Love

><><><
This Illusion
This Paradox
This Question
I sometimes wonder if my feelings are truth
They could just be the hormones
running ramped through my body
But would I not know if I were lying to myself
I want to believe in this "emotion"
Can I even call it that?
The more I feel it the less I want it
It's not something that can be taken back though
I'm just stuck with this eternal curse
of confusion and questioning
Thrown around like a used napkin
after Sunday dinner
Is it even worth chasing
Would you chase trash?
Is it ever meant to be said
Is it ever meant to be genuine
Maybe I'm not meant to know
Just to wonder
while my eyes swell and my ducts fill
Why must these feelings cross my mind
Is this my punishment for my heinous acts
If that's the case then my heart is in a super max
serving life
><><><><><><><><><><><><><><><

My Sisters Keeper

Oh sister,
How I envy you
Tho you are just a babe I envy you
Your naive nature which is the driving force behind
every unpredictable decision you make
is something that I lack
As I observe the uniqueness of your actions it always
pesters my mind how freely one can be even in the
face of unrest
The thickness of your skin is something I may never
achieve no matter how long I hold up this great wall
of diamond
Why must the smallest inconvenience throw my life
into turmoil but for you its just a new adventure to
explore
This persona I portray is not the real me
I want to cry like you do
I want to laugh like you do
I want to feel like you do
I want to live like you do
Although my responsibilities to you
inhibit me from those dreams
The joy that radiates from that whimsical, carefree
smile of yours makes this burden a little lighter
<><><><><><><><><><><><><><><><>

Keeper Of My Sister

Oh sister,
How I envy you
The abilities you have that outshine even the moonlight
That confident nature that always reassures me even in the hardest of times alongside your nurturing aura that never fails to make me feel loved
even when no one else will
Your elegance is something to envy
I stumble and fall at even the slightest inconvenience while you stand tall and face everything head on with your head held high and your shoulders straight and broad
Never have I taken for granted the lessons you have taught me and the valuable gifts you've given me
Even when I didn't want to listen or heed your warnings I valued the impact of your words
You are the reason I can live my truth and be someone you can be truly proud of
The person I have become is because of you
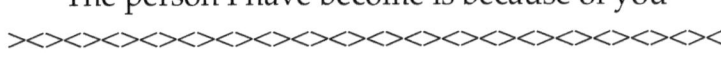
XIII

Betrayal

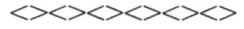

WHY?
Did you even care?
Does the feeling of remorse even trickle in your mind?
Or is this what you wanted
To fill me with
RAGE
ANGER
SADNESS
BETRAYAL
Should I even give you the satisfaction?
How…. How else would you know
I mean you can't read my mind
But you know my heart
Its bled for you everyday

WHY?
Did your heart fall?
Does it still fall?
Never have I wanted to cage it
I just wanted to be the balance
JOY
LOVE
PEACE
COMFORT
Is it too late to have this?
Is…. Is that why?
Was that not us
Am I to blame
Did I even care

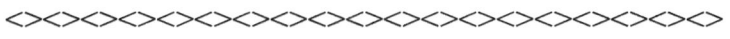

XIV

575 #2

><><><><
The purpose of it
Irrelevant to the theme
Its just complicated
><><><><><><><><
XV

Abandonment

The pit in my stomach will never be filled
It has been imprinted by you
How could you LEAVE?
Will you not tell me the truth or has what I've learned
already been the case
All this time I trusted you, I confided in you
You were my rope pulling me out of my lowest point
Was it all false?
Will you even let me know?
The way you disconnected from my life
was like I was some worn out socket
You made me question myself
Was I part of your scheme?
Were you ever sincere with your words or actions?
Did any of our time mean anything to you?
Your behavior doesn't portray the real you….
Or does it?
The things Ive heard, they scare me
Were you molding me to follow your misleading life
Were you taking advantage of my naive mind to pity
you and your cause
While never once blinking an eye to commit your
heinous acts
Whether I ever hear from you again will not haunt
my life
But your impact has shaped my core

Asthma

The feeling of suffocation
Is something you may never understand
When I expressed my feelings they reached an empty surface denying each and every attempt at an impression
The sheer quickness at which you isolate yourself astounds me every time
Will you allow me to breathe the same air as you?
Is that too much to ask?
The amount of times you've looked my way speaks volumes compared to the meager voice you use to dismiss the notion of US

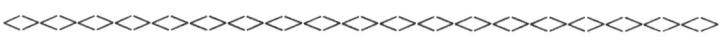

I Took A Walk

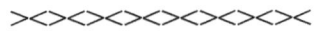

I Took A walk
And felt the chilly breath of the wind against my back
while the sharp eyes of the Sun
peered deep into my skin
I Took A Walk
And heard vibrant music coming from the song birds
while bull frogs sang a low opera
I Took A Walk
And placed my hand into the river to feel the push
and pull of the current
I Took A Walk
And witnessed a mother goose
leading her children to safety
never leaving one behind
I Took A Walk
And got lost in a sea of clouds each making out a
different shape as they passed by
I Took A Walk
And witnessed a single leaf fall from a tree leaving its
family behind to start a new life of unknown
I Took A Walk… And I think I'll take another

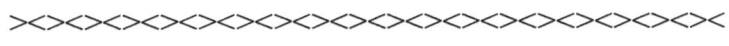

White Fear

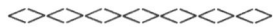
Why do you fear me
What reasons do you have to feel this way towards
me
MY FAMILY Loves me
MY FRIENDS Loves me
MY COMMUNITY Loves me
You call me violent
while you burn my family's property
You call me aggressive
while you scream in my ear calling me NIGGER
You say my music is secular
yet you love to wear my clothes
You say my lips are too big
but you love to "touch up" yours
You tell me to leave
but can you tell me where you're from?
You tell me I'm free
but why is that only when I bow down to your false
idols
You tell me it was all in the past
while you twirl your fallen flag around
What about my persona scares you to the point of
disgracing the sacred texts
you love to reference so much
Do you really fear for your life?
Am I a threat when…

I play with my friends?
I purchase goods from a store
I wear my hood up
I play my music
I walk home
I sit on my porch
I sit in my car
I sit at a coffee shop
I speak my mind
Am I making you uncomfortable? Does the reality of my words disturb you? Does the composition of this piece make you worry?

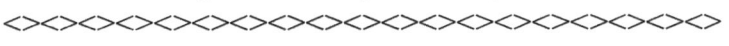

XIX

575 #3

Tightening with force
The pressure it stays applied
Enact the climax
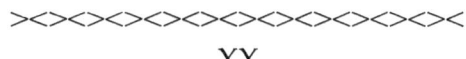
XX

The Back Love Paradox

What is this synergy…this force…this power
that has so much influence
In the workings of my mind
Its never fleeting
Yet won't allow itself to be grasped
I feel it even now coursing through my veins
Rushing but never in a hurry
It likes to take its time as it slowly consumes me
Longing for even a taste of what's in store
I feel as Icarus wanting to fly high and embrace this feeling
NO!
This yearning for the heat of that Sun
Do I want to burn like Icarus?
Do I want to experience his pain?
NO!
But to be enveloped in the
BEAUTY
MAJESTY
ALLURE
EXQUISITENESS
Of this synergy…this force…this…power
I have to be able to endure the blaze
that comes along side it

<><><><><><><><><><><><><><><><>

XXI

Boredom

><><><><
The bright lights intrigued me
They were almost blinding at times
But I stared and stared but was never quite satisfied
This thirst I had could ever be quenched by the lights
No matter how much I turned it up or shaded it, there was never that happy medium
I thought I needed the light but in actuality it needed me
I was the power source
I was the outlet
I was the socket
And while the light shined brighter brighter
I was being drained for my resources
><><><><><><><><><><><><><><
XXII

Heart Cold

Why… why can't I feel what you do
The more I try, the more I get in my own way
I want to connect but I don know how anymore
That might not even be an option for me
The way this is going I may never know completely
how you feel
Am I just a burden
Wasting your time
while you could be out in the world again
Do I even know what I want
I thought I did
I used to not have regrets
but now I see where that's gotten me
<><><><><><><><><><><><><><><><><>
XXIII

Royal Black

<><><><><><><><>
The core of the sun is pale in comparison to the
depths of your nature
Not even Aphrodite could have prepared me for the
ever-changing technicalities of this Godlike being
standing in my view
The plethora of elegance that streams from your body
dominates the atmosphere around you and dispenses
an intoxicating incense
that communicates your confidence
I try not to suffocate in your aura
The air within is thick like the sap of a great oak tree
But I want to swim in your oceans and discover the
inner most parts of your sanctum
With out caution I would leap into the abyss
As long as the drop is filled with remnants of you
<><><><><><><><><><><><><><><><>
XXIV

The Names

><><><><><

HENRY DUMAS
RITA LLOYD
RANDOLPH EVANS
ARTHUR MILLER JR
EULA MAE LOVE
WILLIE TURKS
MICHAEL JEROME STEWART
ELEANOR BUMPERS
MICHEAL GRIFFITH
YVONNE SMALLWOOD
YUSEF KIRRIEM HAWKSINS
MARY MITCHELL
NICHOLAS HEYWARD JR
FRANKIE ANN PERKINS
DANNETTE DANIELS
JAMES BYRD JR
TYISHA SHENEE MILLER
AMADOU DIALLO
MARGARET LaVERNE MITCHELL
LaTANYA HAGERTE
MALCOLM FERGUSON
PRINCE CARMEN JONES JR
PATRICK MOSES DORISMOND
EARL MURRAY
RONALD BEASLEY
TIMOTHY DeWAYNE THOMAS JR
ORLANDO BARLOW
KENDRA SARIE JAMES

ALBERTA SPURRILLE
OUSMANE ZONGO
TIMOTHY STANSBURY JR
HENRY "ACE" GLOVER
JAMES B. BRISSETTE JR
RONALD CURTIS MADISON
KATHRYN JOHNSTON
SEAN BELL
DeAUNTA TERREL FARROW
TARIKA WILSON
OSCAR GRANT III
SHEM WALKER
VICTOR STEEN
KIWANE CARRINGTON
AARON CAMPBELL
STEVEN EUGENE WASHINGTON
AIYANA Mo'NAY STANLEY-JONES
DANROY "DJ" HENRY JR
DERRICK JONES
REGINALD DOUCET
RAHEIM BROWN JR
DEREK WILLIAMS
KENNETH HARDING JR
ALONZO ASHLEY JR
KENNETH CHAMBERLAIN
RAMARLY GRAHAM
MANUAL LEVI LOGGINS JR
TRAYVON MARTIN
RAYMOND LUTHER ALLEN JR
DANTE' LAMAR PRICE
NEHEMIAH LAZAR DILLARD

WENDELL JAMES ALLEN
JERSEY K. GREEN
SHEREESE FRANCIS
REKIA BOYD
KENDREC McDADE
ERVIN JEFFERSON
TAMON ROBINSON
SHARMEL T. EDWARDS
SHANTEL DAVIS
ALESIA THOMAS
CHAVIS CARTER
REYNALDO CUEVAS
NOEL PALANCO
JORDAN RUSSELL DAVIS
MALISSA WILLIAMS
TIMOTHY RUSSELL
DARNISHA HARRIS
SHELLY MARIE FREY
JOHNNIE KAMAHI WARREN
JAMAAL MOORE
KAYLA MOORE
KIMANI "KIKI" GRAY
CLINTON R. ALLEN
DEION FLUDD
KYAM LIVINGSTON
LARRY EUGENE JACKSON JR
CARLOS ALCIS
JONATHAN FERRELL
BARRINGTON "BJ" WILLIAMS
MIRIAM IRIS CAREY
ANDY LOPEZ

JORDAN BAKER
McKENZIE COCHRAN
YVETTE SMITH
GABRIELLA MONIQUE NEVAREZ
VICTOR WHITE III
DONTRE HAMILTON
PEARLIE "MS. SULLY" GOLDEN
ERIC GARNER
TYREE WOODSON
JOHN CRAWFORD III
MICHAEL BROWN JR
EZELL FORD
DANTE PARKER
TANISHA N. ANDERSON
AKAI KAREEM GURLEY
TAMIR RICE
RUMAIN BRISBON
JERAME C. REID
NATASHA McKENNA
JANISHA FONVILLE
TONY TERRELL ROBINSON JR
MEAGAN HOCKADAY
MYA SHAWATZA HALL
PHILLIP GREGORY WHITE
ERIC COURTNEY HARRIS
WALTER LAMAR SCOTT
FREDDIE CARLOS GRAY JR
BRENDON K. GLENN
SANDRA BLAND
SAMUEL VINCENT DuBOSE
INDIA KAGER

JEREMY "BAM BAM" McDOLE
JAMAR O'NEAL CLARK
COREY LAMAR JONES
QUINTONIO LeGRIER
BETTIE "BETTY BOO" JONES
ALTON STERLING
PHILANDO CASTILE
JOSEPH CURTIS MANN
KORRYN GAINES
TERRENCE LeDELL STERLING
TERENCE CRUTCHER
ALFRED OLANGO
DEBORAH DANNER
CHAD ROBERTSON
JORDAN EDWARDS
CHARLEENA CHAVON LYLES
FETUS OF CHARLEENA CHAVON LYLES (14-15 WEEKS)
AARON BAILEY
STEPHON ALONZO CLARK
SAHEED VASSELL
ANTWON ROSE JR
BOTHAM SHEM JEAN
CHINEDU OKOBI
CHARLES "CHOP" ROUNDTREE JR
EMANTIC "EJ" FITZGERALD BRADFORD JR
STERLING LAPREE HIGGINS
JAVIER AMBLER
ELIJAH McCLAIN
ATATIANA KOQUICE JEFFERSON
AHMAUD MARQUEZ ARBERY

MANUEL "MANNIE" ELIJAH ELLIS
BREONNA TAYLOR
MICHAEL BRENT CHARLES RAMOS
DREASJON "SEAN" REED
GEORGE PERRY FLOYD
TONY McDADE
DAVID McATEE
CARLOS CARSON
RAYSHARD BROOKS

XXV

Acknowledgments

The names: Ater, Renée. "IN MEMORIAM: I CAN'T BREATHE." *Renée Ater*, 29 May 2020, www.reneeater.com/on-monuments-blog/tag/list+of+unarmed+black+people+killed+by+police.

Cover Art: Iroshan Fernando

Publisher: KC Publishing

About Khaalil Sutton

What can I say this young man that has taught me so much? Khaalil is the most intelligent, talented and caring person I know. He has shown not only me but others a different way of seeing people and the world.

Taken by Alyssa Lynne White

Khaalil has always walked to his own beat, never feeling the pressure to conform. His faith in God has been essential in what has shaped him into the young man that he is today. Khaalil has always had a close relationship with God and he is not ashamed to let God guide him, he has never been one to succumb to peer pressure.

Khaalil has always had a gift in the arts, he has an ear to mix the rhythm and beats in such a way the music flows through you. He has an eye to be able to design the perfect patterns and colors and have them come together for the perfect picture and the biggest imagination that he can make words flow together like it is nobody's business. He is one of those people that can do anything that he sets his mind to and make it look so easy. He has what we like to call an 'old soul.'

Khaalil has always loved to write and tell "what if" stories and they were always really good and he free styled them. He has finally put those "what if" stories down on paper to share with us. Khaalil writing and self-publishing his first book just shows how focused and determined he is to do things his way on his terms. I see a bright star that God is just getting started with and Khaalil has only just begun entertaining us.

- Titania Sutton

God Bless

www.ingramcontent.com/pod-product-compliance
Lightning Source LLC
Chambersburg PA
CBHW070108100426
42743CB00012B/2696